Math Counts

Sorting

Children's Press®
An Imprint of Scholastic Inc.

About This Series

In keeping with the major goals of the National Council of Teachers of Mathematics, children will become mathematical problem solvers, learn to communicate mathematically, and learn to reason mathematically by using the series Math Counts.

Pattern, Shape, and Size may be investigated first—in any sequence.

Sorting, Counting, and Numbers may be used next, followed by Time, Length, Weight, and Capacity.

—Ramona G. Choos, Professor of Mathematics,
Senior Adviser to the Dean of Continuing Education, Chicago State University;
Sponsor for Chicago Elementary Teachers' Mathematics Club

Author's Note

Mathematics is a part of a child's world. It is not only interpreting numbers or mastering tricks of addition or multiplication. Mathematics is about ideas. These ideas have been developed to explain particular qualities such as size, weight, and height, as well as relationships and comparisons. Yet all too often the important part that an understanding of mathematics will play in a child's development is forgotten or ignored.

Most adults can solve simple mathematical tasks without the need for counters, beads, or fingers. Young children find such abstractions almost impossible to master. They need to see, talk, touch, and experiment.

The photographs and text in these books have been chosen to encourage talk about topics that are essentially mathematical. By talking, the young reader can explore some of the central concepts that support mathematics. It is on an understanding of these concepts that a student's future mastery of mathematics will be built.

—Henry Pluckrose

Math Counts

By Henry Pluckrose

Mathematics Consultant: Ramona G. Choos, Professor of Mathematics

Children's Press®

An Imprint of Scholastic Inc.

What a mix-up! How could you sort it out?

Here are some animals,

some buttons,

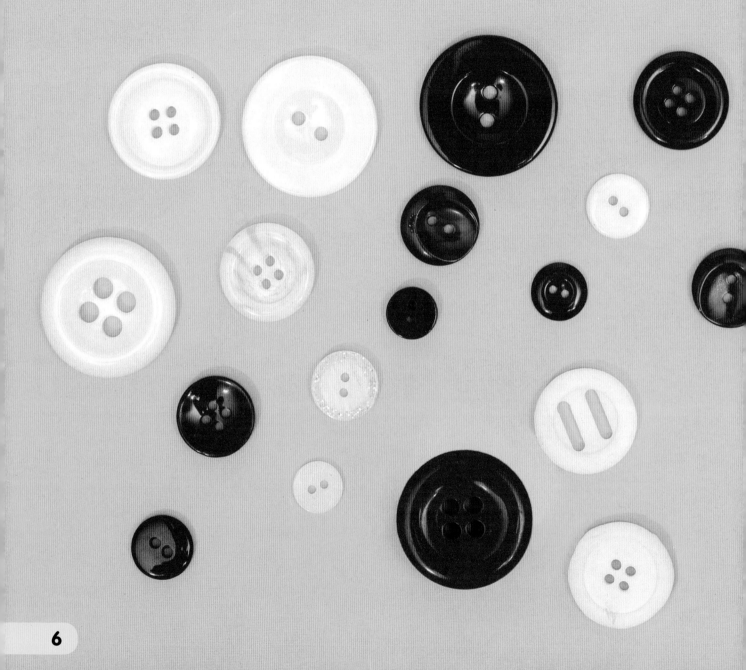

four cars,

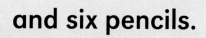

and six pencils.

Look how the animals have been sorted.
Why have they been grouped like this?

The pencils have been sorted in a special way, too.

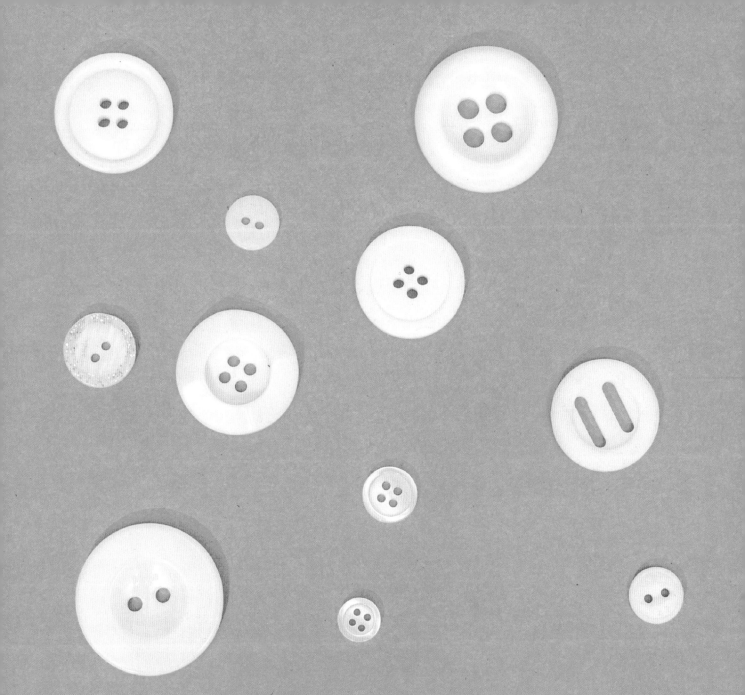

When things are sorted together, they are called a set.
This is a set of buttons.

Everything in this set is red.

What kind of set is this?

How many different ways
could you sort these flowers

and these fruits?

Things that make up a set have something in common. These are all toys

and these things are all found in a bathroom.

What do these things have in common?

And these?

We talk about sets of trains,

Behrens & Michael — My Favorite Book of Numbers
Miller & Mayer — I Love Bunnies
Chanko & Butler — Knock, Knock! Who's There?
Behrens & Butler — I'm Not Tired!
Chanko & Butler — Loud Lion, Quiet Mouse
Miller & Mayer — I Love Puppies
Behrens & Butler — Can You Turn the Page?
Chanko & Highfield — Wave Hello, Wave Bye-Bye
Miller & Mayer — I Love Dinosaurs
Miller & Mayer — I Love Trucks
Falk & Highfield — I See Animal Colors
Behrens & Michael — My Favorite Book of Colors
Behrens & Butler — Bedtime for Rainforest Babies
Falk & Mayer — I Love Kittens
Behrens & Butler — Can You Make a Happy Face?
Chanko & Michael — What Hat Goes With That?

Rookie Toddler®

What HAT Goes With That?

SCHOLASTIC

a set of books,

and even sets of bingo cards.

This is a set of dishes.

This is a container for silverware.
The spaces are used to "set" the knives, forks, and spoons.

When you set a table, each person has a place. What do you notice about each setting?

Sometimes all the things in a set are identical.
Each wheel on a car has to be exactly the same.
Would the extra wheel fit this car?

There is something special about this set of dolls.
How do they fit together?

RADISHES $1.99
MINT 2 FOR $4
ARUGULA 1.49
FRISEE $8.99 LB
ENDIVE

LACINATO KALE $2.99
BASIL $2.99
PARSLEY ROOTS $3.99

LETTUCE $2.99
CARROTS $1.29
ESCAROLE $1.99

If you go into a supermarket you will find vegetables.
They are grouped together.

Are the same kinds of fish grouped together?

What about the bread?
How does this help you find the things you want to buy?

Country Wheat Levain
3 95

Ciabatt
3 75

Seigle
(French Rye)
4 95

Pumpernickle
4 95

Walnut Rye
5 95

Honey Whole Wheat
Pullman
6 00

Rudolf Steiner
7 75

Sunflower
Wholegrain

Multigrain
4 95

eese
nt

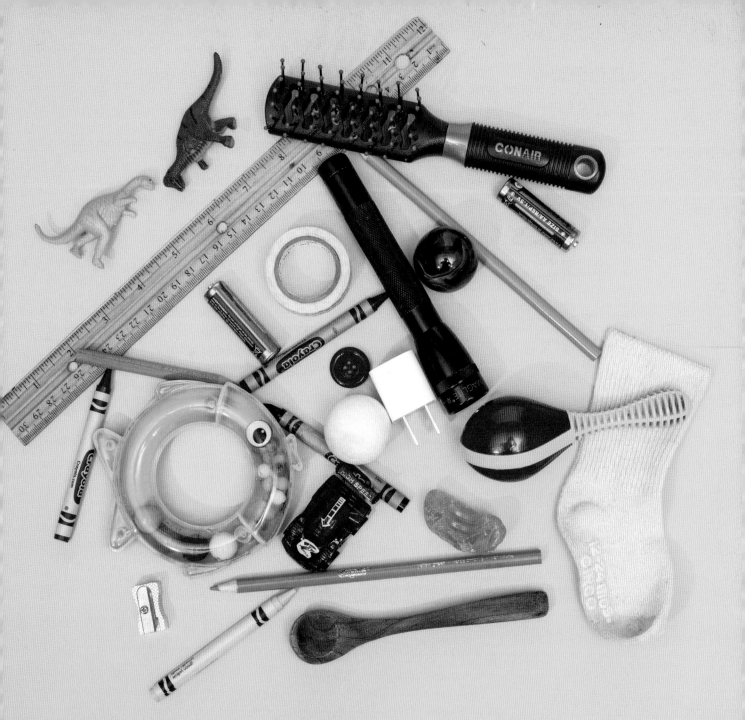

Collect a group of objects.
See how many different ways you can sort them. 31

Index

Reader's Guide

Visit this Scholastic Web site to download the Reader's Guide for this series:
www.factsfornow.scholastic.com Enter the keywords **Math Counts**

Library of Congress Cataloging-in-Publication Data
Names: Pluckrose, Henry, 1931- author. | Choos, Ramona G.
Title: Sorting/by Henry Pluckrose; mathematics consultant, Ramona G. Choos, Professor of Mathematics.
Other titles: Math counts.
Description: Updated edition. | New York, NY: Children's Press, an imprint of Scholastic Inc., 2019. | Series: Math counts | Includes index.
Identifiers: LCCN 2017061286| ISBN 9780531175132 (library binding) | ISBN 9780531135228 (pbk.)
Subjects: LCSH: Set theory—Juvenile literature.
Classification: LCC QA248 .P58 2019 | DDC 511.3/22—dc23

Copyright © The Watts Publishing Group, 2018
Printed in Heshan, China 62

Scholastic Inc., 557 Broadway, New York, NY 10012.

1 2 3 4 5 6 7 8 9 10 R 28 27 26 25 24 23 22 21 20 19

Credits: Photos ©: cover letters: Irina Rogova/Shutterstock; cover-back cover background: R. MACKAY PHOTOGRAPHY, LLC/Shutterstock; 1: Irina Rogova/Shutterstock; 3: Irina Rogova/Shutterstock; 14: Darrell Gulin/Getty Images; 15: ktsimage/iStockphoto; 17: karandaev/iStockphoto; 18: Odua/Dreamstime; 19 top boots: Brooke Becker/Shutterstock; 19 top socks: Evikka/Shutterstock; 19 yellow shoes: poplasen/iStockphoto; 19 white sandals: gsermek/iStockphoto; 19 bottom socks: Stockforlife/Shutterstock; 19 flip flops: Serhii Tsyhanok/iStockphoto; 19 bottom boots: BeylaBalla/iStockphoto; 19 center socks: innature/Shutterstock; 20: Charl Du Toit/Dreamstime; 22: Anan Kaewkhammul/Shutterstock; 23: Roman Yastrebinsky/Shutterstock; 24: ML Harris/Getty Images; 25: Thomas Barwick/Getty Images; 26: Ian Lishman/Getty Images; 27: BrianAJackson/iStockphoto; 28: littleny/iStockphoto; 29: Echo/Getty Images; 30: Premium UIG/Getty Images.

All other images © Bianca Alexis Photography.